# Rachel Carson

## FRIEND OF THE EARTH

# Rachel Carson

## FRIEND OF THE EARTH

by Francene Sabin
illustrated by Yoshi Miyake

This edition published in 2002.

Printed in the United States of America.

10   9   8

*Cover art by Shi Chen.*

*Library of Congress Cataloging-in-Publication Data*

Sabin, Francene.
    Rachel Carson: friend of the earth / by Francene Sabin;
illustrated by Yoshi Miyake.
    p.    cm.
    Summary: Describes the life of the marine biologist and science
writer whose book "Silent Spring" changed the way we look at
pesticides.
    ISBN 0-8167-2821-6 (lib. bdg.)    ISBN 0-8167-4557-9 (pbk.)
    1. Carson, Rachel, 1907-1964—Juvenile literature. 2. Ecologists—
United States—Biography—Juvenile literature. 3. Women
conservationists—United States—Biography—Juvenile literature.
[1. Carson, Rachel, 1907-1964. 2. Environmentalists.
3. Biologists. 4. Science writers.] I. Miyake, Yoshi, ill.
II. Title.
QH31.C33S23  1993
574'.092—dc20
  [B]                       92-5825

# Rachel Carson

## FRIEND OF THE EARTH

Every spring, clouds of annoying mosquitoes appeared over the marshland, so a plane was sent up to spray a pesticide called DDT. The pesticide really worked—it killed almost all of the mosquitoes. This made people happy...for a short time.

Then, birds and fish began to die. There were fewer butterflies that summer. Many birds' eggs didn't hatch. Bumblebees and grasshoppers began to disappear. All this happened because DDT was in the water, in the soil, on trees and shrubs and grasses.

This was happening all around the world. Cows grazed on grass poisoned by pesticides, and traces of these chemicals were found in their milk. People drank milk and ate meat, vegetables, and fish—all carrying traces of pesticides.

Earth was being poisoned and nobody paid attention. Then, in 1962, a book appeared. It was called *Silent Spring* by Rachel L. Carson. Like the rings made by a pebble dropped into a pool, the book's message spread. It showed us that our world is doomed if we continue to poison it with dangerous chemicals.

Today, we know how fragile our Earth can be. Today, we know the words *environment, ecology, endangered species, food chain,* and *balance of nature.* For this knowledge, the world must thank Rachel Carson.

When she wrote *Silent Spring,* Carson felt that there was an important story to tell. She knew that people didn't have to be scientists to understand. They just needed to be told things in an honest and clear way. Honest and clear—those are the words that describe Rachel Carson's writing and thinking, and the person she was.

9

Rachel Louise Carson was born on May 27, 1907, in Springdale, near Pittsburgh, Pennsylvania. Her parents, Maria and Robert Carson, already had two children: eight-year-old Robert, Jr. and ten-year-old Marian.

The Carsons' house was in the country. Mrs. Carson cooked the family's meals on a wood-burning stove. Like many homes in the early 1900s, the house had no gas or electricity, and no running water. The Carsons used oil lamps or candles for lighting. Their only heat came from a fireplace in the parlor.

Rachel's family kept chickens, a cow, a few pigs, and some rabbits. They also grew their own vegetables. Like the early pioneers, the Carsons kept their food fresh in a springhouse. Rachel's father built a small enclosure of stone and wood over an ice-cold spring that bubbled up from the ground near the house. This natural refrigerator kept the food cold and also protected it from wild animals. And the frosty, clear water was delicious to drink.

The Carsons owned sixty-five acres of land, most of it woods. It was natural, unspoiled, and beautiful. Marian, Robert, and Rachel loved to wander in the woodland world. They saw all kinds of animals and birds. They ate apples from their orchard and fresh vegetables from their garden. The children fished in the sparkling brook that wound through the woods. They picked wild raspberries and huckleberries, eating almost as many as they brought home for pies and jams.

The Carsons respected all the life on their land. Mrs. Carson didn't even like to kill insects. Whenever she found a spider or beetle in the house, she scooped it up and carried it outside. "Insects mean us no harm," Mrs. Carson told the children. "And we have no reason to harm them."

13

When Rachel was grown up, she remembered her mother's example. As a scientist, Rachel Carson often collected live specimens for study. But she did not throw them away when her work was done. Instead, she kept the fish, clams, crabs, and other creatures alive in a bucket of seawater. As soon as she could, she returned them to their natural habitat.

Mrs. Carson showed Rachel many things in the woods and fields around their house. They watched chipmunks dash around, collecting acorns for the winter. They saw golden butterflies landing lightly on wildflower blossoms, and birds building nests and feeding their chirping babies.

"Close your eyes, Rachel," Mrs. Carson said. "Listen carefully." There was a symphony of sounds around them—singing birds, whirring insects, rustling leaves.

15

Maria McLean Carson loved to teach. She was never too busy to answer questions, to read aloud, or to go on a "discovery" walk through the woods. Mr. Carson's job with a power company kept him away from home a lot. Robert, Jr. and Marian were busy with school and friends and hobbies. Mrs. Carson and Rachel were often left to themselves.

Mrs. Carson had once been a schoolteacher. She graduated from the Washington (Pennsylvania) Seminary in 1887, where she won special honors in Latin. She was also a talented musician who composed music and taught piano and singing.

But when Maria McLean married Robert Carson, she had to stop teaching. In those days, female teachers were forced to leave their jobs if they got married. It was considered shameful for a wife to work outside her home. Many businesses refused to hire women at all.

An unmarried, educated woman could be a teacher, office assistant, or librarian. A married woman, educated or not, had no career choices. She was expected to stay home and keep house. If she needed to earn money, she had to do it at home. But there were not many ways to do that.

The Carson family was always short of money. Rachel's mother earned a little by giving piano lessons in the parlor. But Mrs. Carson did not have many students, because their house was too far away for most children to come for lessons. Instead, she poured her talent and dreams into Rachel.

When Rachel started first grade, she was far ahead of the other children. She had the best grades in the class. But she also had the worst attendance record at Springdale Elementary School, because she was often sick with a cold or sore throat.

Whenever Rachel missed school she did all her homework, and more. If she asked her mother to explain something, Mrs. Carson always said, "That's an interesting question. Let's see if you can find the answer and explain it to me." Then Rachel looked through books, hunting for answers to "How?" and "Why?" That way Rachel learned to do research and to think things through.

Rachel also loved to write. She wrote her first "book" when she was in second grade. It was about animals, birds, fish, and bugs. Each page had a drawing and a short poem. Her drawings were quite good. They really looked like the mice, frogs, and other living things Rachel saw in the woods.

Rachel was very proud of her book, and gave it to her father as a birthday present. Mr. Carson was full of praise for his daughter. "What a wonderful book!" he said. "You're a fine writer, Rachel. I'm so proud of you!"

Every month, Rachel read a children's magazine called *St. Nicholas.* It had stories, poems, puzzles, games, and drawings. There was also a section for pieces written by young readers. The best of these contributions were awarded gold and silver badges.

When she was eight years old, Rachel began to send poems and stories to *St. Nicholas.* They were always returned with kind words. Then, in September 1918, Rachel received a ten-dollar check from the magazine. It was for a story called "A Battle in the Clouds."

Rachel's story was about a World War One airplane battle. In 1918, the United States was at war with Germany, and Rachel's brother, Robert, was in the U.S. Army Aviation Service, training to be a pilot. One time, when he was home on leave, Robert told his family about a brave fellow airman. Rachel wrote the story in her own words and sent it to *St. Nicholas*. It won the silver badge.

Rachel kept writing and sending stories to *St. Nicholas*. Every day, on the way home from school, she opened the mailbox hopefully. Her efforts were rewarded in February 1919 with a gold badge story, and then another in August of that same year. Now she had thirty dollars in the bank for her college fund. Best of all, there was her name—Rachel L. Carson—in the magazine!

Everyone said a writer had to learn about a lot of things. So Rachel made up her mind to do just that. In her high-school yearbook, her classmates wrote:

> Rachel's like the mid-day sun
> Always very bright
> Never stops studying
> 'Til she gets it right.

However, there was still time for fun. Rachel was on the field hockey team at school, and played the piano for family sing-alongs on weekends. And whenever she could, she wandered through the fields and woods.

In 1925, when she was eighteen, Rachel graduated from high school. She had very high grades and won a college scholarship to the Pennsylvania College for Women (PCW), in nearby Pittsburgh.

PCW was a small school, with just three hundred students. Mrs. Carson said, "It's perfect, Rachel dear. The classes will be small, and every student will get a lot of attention. And you'll be able to come home any time you want."

The college *was* ideal for young Rachel. She dived into her studies, and into her new life away from home. As a freshman, she took courses in math, music, history, French, and English. She also became a reporter for the school newspaper, *The Arrow*. Carson wanted to become a professional writer, and practiced her writing every day.

*Professor Mary Skinker*

In Carson's sophomore year, she had to take a course in biology. This class changed her whole life. Professor Mary Scott Skinker, her biology teacher, was tough. Skinker's students had to do a lot of textbook reading and laboratory experiments. Nobody passed her class without studying hard. And nobody got an A without really earning it.

In those days, many people said that women weren't able to be real scientists. Professor Skinker didn't agree. She said, "Give women the same work, make the same demands, and they will do just as well as men." For Rachel Carson, that was more than true. She proved it by getting an A for the class. In addition, the biology course gave her a new goal. She still loved writing, but she decided to become a biologist.

For the rest of her college years, Carson took many science courses. She also worked on her own projects. Carson's main interest was the animal life around her. She studied turtles, frogs, grasshoppers, crayfish, and other small local creatures. And, of course, she continued to write.

In May 1929, Rachel Carson graduated from college with high honors. She was awarded a summer study fellowship at the Marine Biological Laboratory in Woods Hole, Massachusetts. And she was also given a one-year scholarship to Johns Hopkins University, in Baltimore, Maryland. There, she planned to study for a master's degree in zoology. (Zoology is the branch of biology that deals with the animal kingdom and its members.)

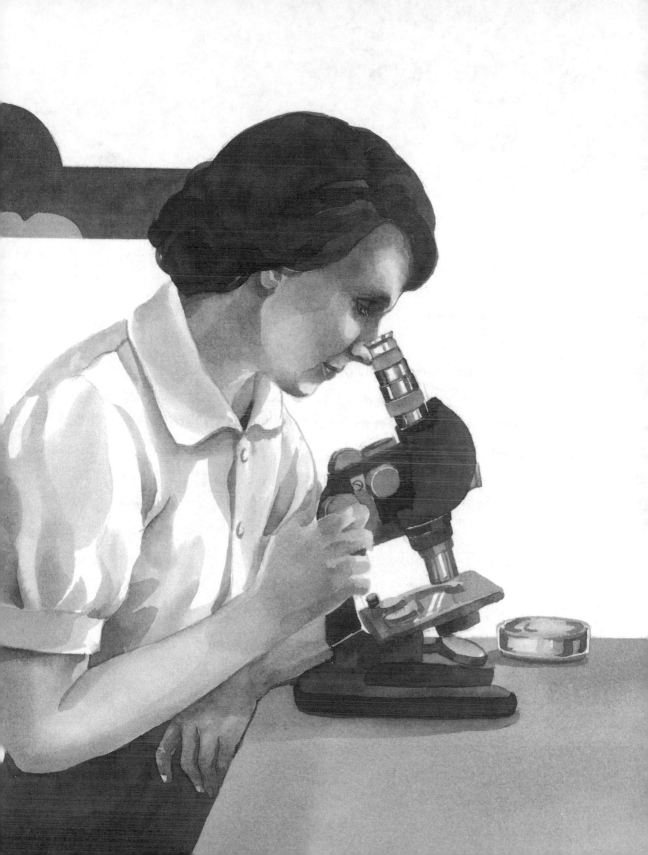

Rachel Carson's first summer at Woods Hole was like finding a treasure. She had read about the ocean all her life, but she had never seen it. Now she had two whole months on Cape Cod, right at the edge of the Atlantic. Here she discovered sand dunes and beach grasses, gulls and sandpipers, crabs and clams, and the ocean itself, with its rolling surf and breakers crashing to the shore. For Carson, it was instant love. "Someday," she promised herself, "I will live close to the ocean."

By the end of the summer of 1929, Carson had no doubts about her future. She was going to be a marine biologist, and study the life of the sea. But first it was on to Johns Hopkins to study for her master's degree.

Rachel Carson's graduate work was very hard. She spent many hours doing library research. And she spent many more in the laboratory, bent over a microscope. There was no time for a social life or sports. Sometimes she was so busy, she even forgot to eat lunch.

When school had begun, in the fall of 1929, the Carsons sold their Pennsylvania home and moved to Baltimore. They bought a small house near the Johns Hopkins campus. At this time, the Great Depression was just beginning. Life was difficult throughout the world. In the United States, factories closed and millions of people were out of work. It was just as bad for farmers. A few years of no rain turned rich farms into dusty wastelands. Like many people, the Carsons had a tough time paying their bills.

Rachel Carson felt lucky to have her scholarship. It paid for her first year's schooling. When summer came, she worked as a teaching assistant in the university's summer school. The title "teaching assistant" sounded a lot more important than it was. Carson washed laboratory glassware, cleaned tables, and set up equipment for each class. But the job brought in money, and she welcomed it.

When Carson's scholarship ended, she still needed two more years of schooling to complete her degree. Those years meant one grinding day after another, because Carson needed to work while she attended school. One of her jobs was as a teaching assistant in biology at Johns Hopkins. For a second job, she was a lab assistant to one of her professors. And her third job was as a part-time assistant in the zoology department at the University of Maryland. The Maryland job was a thirty-five-mile bus trip each way. That took precious hours out of Carson's week. But she needed the money to pay for school. And she was determined not to give up.

Years later, a male classmate remembered Carson's tough schedule. "We used to feel sorry for Rachel," he said, "and we told her so. In those days, we didn't think a woman was up to being a scientist. And we certainly didn't think a woman could work two or three jobs, go to school, commute back and forth, get top grades—and survive."

Carson did more than survive. She earned excellent marks and received her master's degree in zoology in the spring of 1932. For the next three years, she struggled to earn a living at part-time jobs. Meanwhile, she kept applying for full-time scientific work. But museums, universities, and industries did not hire female scientists in those days. Things were not much easier for Rachel Carson in the 1930s than they had been for her mother forty years earlier.

The Depression continued to hit the Carsons. Robert, Jr. lost his job and came to live with the family. So did Marian and her two children. Robert earned a little money repairing radios. Mr. Carson had a small pension. But Rachel was the main support of the family.

Mr. Carson died in July of 1935, and his pension stopped. Now Rachel needed a full-time job. When the next U.S. Government Civil Service examination was given, Carson took it. She was the only woman applicant, and she received the highest test score. Soon after, she was hired by the Department of the Interior as a junior aquatic biologist in the Bureau of Fisheries. Her salary was $2,000 a year.

Carson's title was "biologist," but she didn't work in a laboratory or aboard a scientific research ship. She wrote radio scripts about fish and other marine life. These were part of a series called "Romance Under the Waters." Again, Carson's talent shone through. The scripts were so good, the Bureau published them as a booklet. Carson also earned extra money writing articles for the *Baltimore Sun* newspaper and for magazines.

In September 1937, the *Atlantic Monthly Magazine* published an article by Carson called "Undersea." It introduced the reader to the sights, sounds, tastes, and feelings of ocean creatures, and asked the readers to imagine living under the sea. It was a very unusual article.

"Undersea" became the basis of *Under the Sea Wind*, Carson's first book. Reviewers everywhere praised the book, but it was published in November 1941, one month before the United States entered World War Two. People were not interested in reading a book about the ocean while the world was at war.

During World War Two, the Bureau of Fisheries, now called the Fish and Wildlife Service, urged Americans to eat more fish. Rachel Carson's job was to write a series of booklets about freshwater and saltwater fish and shellfish. She described how they lived, how they were caught, and how to prepare and serve them.

The booklets were well-written and very useful. They were quoted all the time in magazines and newspapers, and on radio programs. But Rachel Carson got no recognition for her fine work. All the credit went to the Fish and Wildlife Service.

After the war ended in 1945, Carson was named editor of a new series of twelve booklets called "Conservation in Action." She wrote several of the booklets herself. The series told about wildlife in the United States. Each booklet was full of colorful illustrations and fascinating facts about plants, animals, insects, and the land itself.

As she worked on "Conservation in Action,"
Carson began to worry about the environment. In
her introduction to the series, she wrote, "Wild
creatures, like men, must have a place to live. As
civilization creates cities, builds highways, and
drains marshes, it takes away, little by little, the
land that is suitable for wildlife. And as their
spaces for living dwindle, the wildlife populations
themselves decline."

She also wrote, "For all the people, the preservation of wildlife and wildlife habitat means also the preservation of the basic resources of the earth, which men, as well as animals, must have in order to live. Wildlife, water, forests, grasslands—all are part of man's essential environment."

But at that time, even Carson did not realize how serious the problem was. In 1948, her greatest scientific interest and her greatest pleasure was the ocean. Since her first trip to Woods Hole, in 1929, she had one ambition. She wanted to write a book about the sea that would be scientific, interesting, and understood by everyone.

In 1949, Carson took a leave of absence from her job. She studied the Atlantic Ocean from a Fish and Wildlife survey ship. She went deep-sea diving off the Florida coast. She also examined many forms of sea life in the laboratory. Finally, in July of 1950, her book, *The Sea Around Us,* was finished.

Even before the book was published, it won science awards, and sections of it appeared in *The New Yorker Magazine*. When *The Sea Around Us* went on sale in bookstores in 1951, it was a sensation. For more than a year and a half it was on *The New York Times* best-seller list. Many magazines reprinted chapters and condensed parts of the book. It was translated into many languages and quoted around the world.

Rachel Carson was famous. *Under the Sea Wind* was reissued, and also became a best seller. Hollywood made a documentary film of *The Sea Around Us*, and it won an Academy Award. After years of struggling, Carson quit her job to write full-time. And she was able to afford another dream. She bought land on the coast of Maine and had a cottage built, facing the sea.

There, Carson worked on her next book, *The Edge of the Sea*. It was all about the shoreline: the plants and animals, the insects, the shifting sands. Carson was especially interested in tide pools, the protected pockets of shallow water where many sea creatures live.

Bob Hines, Carson's illustrator at the Fish and Wildlife Service, spent many days at the tide pools with her. Carson wanted the book's drawings to make all the creatures look alive and natural. Hines's fine drawings did that. They helped to make *The Edge of the Sea* a huge success when it came out in 1955.

The next few years brought many changes to
Carson's life. Her niece, Marjorie, died, and
Rachel adopted her five-year-old son, Roger.
Not long after that, her mother died. It was a
sad time, but her writing and Roger kept Carson
busy. He was a bright little boy, and raising him
made her very happy. She wanted his life to be
wonderful, and she began to worry about the
world of the future—his world.

Carson wanted to write a short article about the dangers of pesticides. She started to do research and was horrified by what she learned. The story was too big to tell in an article, so Carson decided to write a book. As a scientist, she wanted it to be accurate. As a writer, she wanted her words to be clear. As a human being who cared about the future and all the children like Roger, she wanted people to pay attention.

Rachel Carson was a very private person. She didn't like to call attention to herself. She didn't find it easy to write harsh words about industries and governments. But now she had to speak out, even if it made people angry and shattered the privacy she treasured.

When *Silent Spring* was published in 1962, it rocked the world like a giant earthquake. Rachel Carson's words were clear and simple. She described what happens when a chemical pesticide like DDT is used. She told about the effects of pesticides on fish and wildlife, on farms, on the food we eat, on our health.

Reactions to the book were strong and immediate. Articles appeared, attacking her as a kook, a hysterical woman, a fanatic opposed to progress, and a non-scientist. Other articles praised her courage for speaking out. But the most important result was that people *did* begin to pay attention to the dangers Carson wrote about.

President John F. Kennedy appointed a committee to study pesticides. Rachel Carson met with the committee and testified before the United States Congress. Secretary of the Interior Stewart L. Udall said, "Rachel Carson alerted us to the subtle dangers of an Age of Poisons. She made us realize that we had allowed our fascination with chemicals to override our wisdom in their use."

Colleges and universities gave Rachel Carson honorary degrees. She was elected to the American Academy of Arts and Sciences, and honored by scientific groups and government agencies. Much of her time was spent making speeches, alerting the world to the threats against the environment.

Carson looked tired and pale during these busy months. Some people thought her heavy schedule was the reason. But her close friends knew the truth. Carson had been suffering from cancer since the spring of 1960. Surgery and radiation treatments helped a little, but not enough. She grew weaker and suffered a heart attack in 1963. Knowing the end was near, she retired to her beach cottage in Maine. There, close to the sea she loved so deeply, Rachel Carson died on April 14, 1964.

After her death, a *New York Times* editor wrote, "She was a biologist, not a crusader, but the power of her knowledge and the beauty of her language combined to make Rachel Carson one of the most influential women of our time."

47

# INDEX